CATMAS CAROLS

CATMAS CAROLS

LAURIE LOUGHLIN
Illustrations by GEMMA CORRELL

CHRONICLE BOOKS
SAN FRANCISCO

The author and publisher have made every reasonable attempt
to determine that the songs parodied in this work are in the public domain.

Library of Congress Cataloging-in-Publication Data

Loughlin, Laurie.
 Catmas Carols / Laurie Loughlin.
    pages cm
 ISBN 978-1-4521-1246-6
1. Cats—Humor. 2. Carols, English—Humor. 3. Christmas—Humor. 4. Parodies. I.
Correll, Gemma, illustrator. II. Title.
 PN6231.C23L68 2013
 818'.5402—dc23

                                        2012045218

Manufactured in China

Designed by Ryan Diaz

10 9 8 7 6 5 4 3 2

Chronicle Books LLC
680 Second Street
San Francisco, California 94107
www.chroniclebooks.com

In memory of Max, beloved friend.

I WOULD LIKE TO THANK

MY PARENTS, RICHARD and LAURA LOUGHLIN,
for placing my childhood rocking chair next to the
record player and encouraging my love of songs;

MY EDITOR, EMILIE SANDOZ, for making this book
new again;

GEMMA CORRELL for her endearing illustrations;

MY FRIENDS, JOHN RUMBLE, CHRISTA SHREFFLER,
and BOB REDDIG for coming up with some of
the parody titles;

and ALL CATS (especially REIKO and NED) for being
the splendid individuals they are.

CONTENTS

🐾

WE THREE CATS OF ORIENT ARE

"WE THREE KINGS OF ORIENT ARE"

We three cats of Orient are
Terrified to get in the car.
Why go out for celebrating?
We'll stay right where we are. Oooh—

> CHORUS:
> Home is heaven. Home is good.
> Home is where we get our food.
> Why go out for Christmas parties?
> Frankly we're not in the mood.

We're not happy with a trip yet.
Seems they always end at the vet.
These excursions are diversions
We'd just as soon forget. Oooh—

> (Repeat CHORUS)

We three cats are Siamese,
Himalayan, and Tonkinese.
Bring us gifts of meat with gravy
And mild kinds of cheese. Oooh—

> (Repeat CHORUS)

OH, CHRISTMAS TREE

"O TANNENBAUM"

Oh, Christmas Tree!
Oh, Christmas Tree!
Your ornaments shine
    temptingly.
I want to whack them with
    my paw
And grab them when they
    hit the floor.
Oh, Christmas Tree!
Oh, Christmas Tree!
Your ornaments shine
    temptingly.

AWAKE IN A CAT BED

"AWAY IN A MANGER"

Awake in a cat bed,
She can't go to sleep.
She's thinking of cat toys
That she'd like to keep.
She's seen them in catalogs
And on TV,
And she's left her Christmas list
Pinned to the tree.

A catnip-filled heart and
A long piece of string,
A large kitty condo,
With everything,
A stocking with treats and
A brush for her fur,
She's hoping that Santa
Will bring these for her.

THE FIRST
MEOW

The first meow,
The angels did say,
Was to certain white Persians
On rugs where they lay,
On rugs where they
Lay trying to sleep,
Having dreams about cat life
That were so deep.
Meow, meow, meow, meow.
They'll get to do what they
    want, somehow.

WRECK
THE HALLS

"DECK THE HALLS"

Wreck the halls with two cats running,
    Fa-la-la-la-la…la-la-la-la.
Fur goes flying, lamps get done in,
    Fa-la-la-la-la…la-la-la-la.
Tumbling swiftly down the stairway,
    Fa-la-la, la-la-la, la, la, la.
Woe to those who get in their way,
    Fa-la-la-la-la…la-la-la-la.

I SAW
THREE CATS

"I SAW THREE SHIPS"

I saw three cats prance merrily
On Christmas Day, on Christmas Day,
I saw three cats prance merrily
On Christmas Day, in the morning.

They played a game of hide-and-seek
On Christmas Day, on Christmas Day,
They played a game of hide-and-seek
Oh Christmas Day, in the morning.

And rolled around on the floor with glee
On Christmas Day, on Christmas Day,
And rolled around on the floor with glee
On Christmas Day, in the morning.

Greta, Max, and Penelope
On Christmas Day, on Christmas Day,
Greta, Max, and Penelope
On Christmas Day, in the morning

To watch them brings such joy to me
On Christmas Day, on Christmas Day,
To watch them brings such joy to me
On Christmas Day, in the morning.

OH, COME
ALL YE FURFUL

"OH, COME ALL YE FAITHFUL"

Oh, come all ye furful,
Hungry and well-rested,
Oh, come ye, oh, come ye to
The master bedroom.

Come and behold them
Snoring loudly 'neath the sheets,
For now it's time to wake them,
For now it's time to wake them,
For now it's time to wake them
On this Christmas morn.

Meow, choirs of felines,
Meow in expectation.
Meow till you get your Mom
And Dad out of bed.
Glory to food
In the cat dish.
Oh, come let us enjoy it.
Oh, come let us enjoy it.
Oh, come let us enjoy it,
Breakfast at last!

GOOD CATS
IN THE HOUSE

Good cats in the house are bad
When their Mom's not looking,
Stick their noses everywhere
Just to see what's cooking.
When their claws need polishing,
Shred the couch and love seat.
They don't heed admonishing,
But their misdeeds repeat!

Good cats in the house are sad
When they feel neglected.
They will yowl without respite
Or act cool and affected.
Special love at Christmastime
Is what they require,
That we pet them ceaselessly,
Their good looks admire!

HALLELUJAH POUR US

"HALLELUJAH CHORUS"

Hallelujah! Hallelujah!

The food bag is tilted. Hallelujah!

Hallelujah! Hallelujah!

Food cascading, coming towards us. Hallelujah!
Is it Purina Chow? Perhaps Meow Mix?

Hallelujah! Hallelujah! Hallelujah! Hallelujah!

Alpo or Friskies? All have their taste kicks.

Hallelujah! Hallelujah! Hallelujah! Hallelujah!

And we shall eat forever and ever.
And we shall eat forever and ever.

Hail, Nine Lives,

Hallelujah! Hallelujah! Hallelujah! Hallelujah!

And Happy Cat.

Hallelujah! Hallelujah! Hallelujah! Hallelujah!

Whiskas jives

Hallelujah! Hallelujah! Hallelujah! Hallelujah!

With my habitat.

Hallelujah! Hallelujah! Hallelujah! Hallelujah!

Hallelujah!

IT CAME UPON
A MIDNIGHT CAT

"IT CAME UPON A MIDNIGHT CLEAR"

It came upon a midnight cat
Whose fur was black and bold,
As he sat under the carport in
December though it was cold,
That he was lord of his backyard.
The neighbor cats would agree,
For, when he hisses, they turn and leave
His yard immediately.

COLLAR BELLS

"JINGLE BELLS"

CHORUS:
Collar bells, collar bells,
Ringing 'round the block,
Christmas Eve is party time,
And we cats like to rock.
Collar bells, collar bells,
Ringing 'round the block,
Christmas Eve is party time,
We're counting down the clock.

We wait out on the porch
And sing amewsing songs.
We know that Santa Claws
Will be here before long.
The chimney has been swept
To ease his passage down.
We'll entertain the reindeer
While he puts the presents 'round.
    Oh,

(Repeat CHORUS)

Our families are asleep,
But not we watchful cats.
While waiting we engage
In elementary spats,
Deciding who'll be boss
And shake ol' Santa's hand.
This holiday excitement's
Almost more than we can stand.
Oh,

(Repeat CHORUS)

GO, SMELL IT AT THE FOUNTAINS

"GO, TELL IT ON THE MOUNTAIN"

When I was a kitten,
    my Mama mewed to me,
"You'll have to find your food yourself
    when there's no other way.
Go, smell it at the fountains,
Out on the docks, in market stalls.
Go, smell it at the fountains.
Our Christmas fish is spawned."

Now I am in charge of
    The Christmas feast for cats.
They know that I'm an expert sniff
    At finding this and that.
"Go, smell it at the fountains,
Out on the docks, in market stalls.
Go, smell it at the fountains,
Our Christmas fish is spawned."

BARK! THE NEIGHBORS' DOGS WILL SOUND

"HARK! THE HERALD ANGELS SING"

Bark! The neighbors' dogs will sound
When they see us spin around.
They can really make it hard
For cats to play in the yard.

Canine cousins are a puzzle.
Santa, please bring each a muzzle.
We can't wait for the time when
Silent nights are here again.

Bark! The neighbors' dogs will sound.
May Christmas peace and love abound!

INSISTENT CATS, REJOICE

"GOOD CHRISTIAN MEN, REJOICE"

Insistent cats, rejoice
With rubs and purrs and voice.
It's time to cuddle close
With those you love the most.
Jump on laps and sideways lie.
Stretch your paws out toward
    the sky.
Petting is such bliss.
You were born for this.

O! LITTLE TOWN
OF CAT MAYHEM

"O! LITTLE TOWN OF BETHLEHEM"

O! Little town of Cat Mayhem,
What mischiefs among you lie?
They look angelic in their sleep,
But there's nothing they won't try.
And in the dark night shineth
Alert, translucent eyes
As they attack the Christmas stockings
Carrying off the prize.

WHAT CHAIR
IS THIS?

"WHAT CHILD IS THIS"

What chair is this
Where I can rest
On Mama's (Papa's) lap lie sleeping,
Or watch cars go
On the street below
While through the curtains I'm peeping?

CHORUS:
This, this is my favorite chair.
Come morning, evening, you'll find me there.
This, this is my favorite chair,
My throne, my place of contentment.

So bring me sunshine
And bring me love.
I need you so I'm not lonely.
The king (queen) of cats,
I know I'm that,
And no other cat will dethrone me.

CHORUS

OH, HOLD
ME RIGHT

"O HOLY NIGHT"

Oh, hold me right.
Your grasp has got me keeling.
It's whine and squirm time
When you pick me up.
Long have I tried
To let you know my feeling,
That when you lift me,
My life you disrupt!

I'd rather trot
And go about my business.
The grip you've got's
Not popular with me.

Put me down, please.
I need to see the turkey.
Oh, sight divine,
Even though I'm now airborne.
Oh, sight divine!
Let me go! This bird is mine!

GOD REST YE MERRY, KITTY CATS

"GOD REST YE MERRY, GENTLEMEN"

God rest ye merry, kitty cats,
Let nothing you dismay.
Remember, lots of yummy food
Is served on Christmas Day,
To save us all from hungry tummies,
Hip, hip, hip hooray!
Oooh, tidings of catnip and joy,
Catnip and joy.
Oooh, tidings of catnip and joy.

HERE WE COME
A-TAIL-SNIFFING

"HERE WE COME A-WASSAILING"

Here we come a-tail-sniffing.
We do it every day.
I know you, but I must be sure,
And it's the only way.

Don't get mad. Don't run off.
Please don't swat me with your paw,
And I'll groom you and play with you all
    through the New Year.
I'll play with you all through the New Year.

We two cats live in this house
And get along so well.
When eyesight's not enough ID,
We use our sense of smell.

Please don't hiss. Please don't growl
When my nose goes on the prowl,
And I'll groom you and play with you all
    through the New Year.
I'll play with you all through the New Year.

JOY TO
THE WORLD

Joy to the World, 'cause cats are here.
They fill all hearts with love.
Let everyone prepare them food
And let them eat their fill,
And let them eat their fill,
And let, and let them eat their fill.